Where Did GRANDAD Go?

Catherine House and Honor Ayres

Pauline
BOOKS & MEDIA
Boston

Every Saturday afternoon, Megan went to visit her granny. Granny's house smelled of cakes baking in the oven. Granny grew yellow and pink tulips, but she loved yellow tulips best.

Granny gave big hugs!

"It's a beautiful day, Megan," said Granny. "Shall we go for a walk and put these tulips on Grandad's grave?"
Megan took the tulips. They were all yellow.
"These are very pretty, Granny," she said. "But can I choose some pink ones just from me?"

Granny smiled.
"Of course you
can, Megan. But
watch out for that
bee!"

"Look at the robin!" whispered Megan. "What's he doing?"
"He's trying to catch a worm," said Granny.

8

"The birds are busy now. They are happy that winter is over.
And look over here: a whole hillside of primroses!"

9

"Oh, Granny!" said Megan. "Look! There's a dead bird."

"It's a sparrow, Megan. A poor tired sparrow that won't have to worry about finding food anymore."

"But that's so sad, Granny. Why did it have to die?"

"Everything that is born has to die one day. It is sad. But that little sparrow is in God's hands. God cares about every sparrow that falls to the ground. He cares even more about you and me. We are very special to God; he even knows how many hairs are on our heads."

"Here we are. Do you remember where Grandad's grave is?"

"Yes, I can see it!" said Megan. "Oh look, Granny. There's a little mouse!"

"Please, will you arrange the flowers for me, Megan—your pink tulips and my yellow ones? Grandad always loved spring flowers."

"Granny, does God live here—with Grandad and the flowers and the field mouse?" asked Megan. "Is this where people go when they die?"

"God is here, Megan, with us and with the creatures he has made. And this is where Grandad's body is buried and where my body will come, too. But Grandad isn't here now. When he died, Grandad went to a new home in God's house."

"Then does God live here in the church, Granny?" asked Megan. "Is this God's house?"

"God is here too, Megan," replied Granny. "But it's not really where he lives. God is in heaven. In heaven, there's a special place for Grandad. God has plenty of room there for everyone who loves him."

"What is it like where God lives?" Megan asked.

"I don't know what it looks like, but I do know it's a very happy place. No one will be sick there or feel pain.

"No one will be sad or lonely. No one will need to cry ever again."

Granny paused for a moment.

"I miss Grandad, Megan," she said.

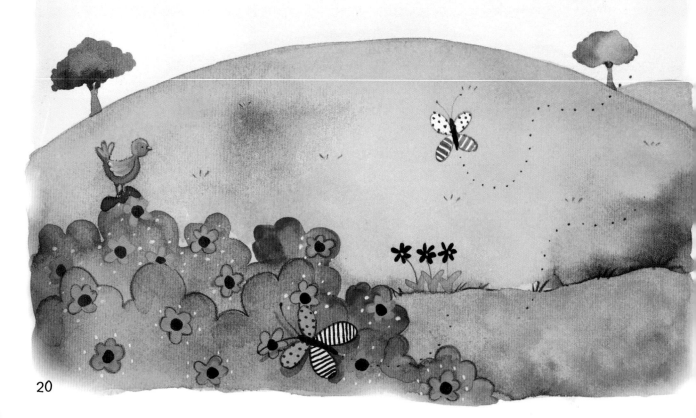

"Someday I will go to that special place in God's house, just as Grandad did."

"I don't want you to die, Granny," said Megan. "I want you to stay here with me forever."

"I know, Megan. And I don't want to leave you either. But my body is getting old and worn out—like the sparrow we saw. God cares for me and he has promised to give me a new body, as well as a special place to live in his house."

"Can you visit people in heaven, Granny? Will I be able to visit you?"

"Megan, I am near the end of my life's journey; sometimes my life has been very happy; sometimes it has been difficult. But you are just at the beginning! There are many exciting things for you to do yet!

"But when the time is right, at the end of your journey, there will be a special room in God's house ready for you, too."

25

"I will miss you, Granny, when you go away."

"Of course you will, Megan. We always feel sad when someone dies. We miss people we love when they are no longer here. That's the time to remember all the good things about them."

"You can remember the walks we went on and the smell of cakes baking in my kitchen. You can remember the animals we watched and how God loves us even more than the sparrows. You can remember me when you *see* yellow tulips in springtime.

"You can remember the lovely times we have had together and you can thank God. And you can think of me, no longer old and tired, but happy in that *special* place in God's house."

House, Catherine.
Where did grandad go? / Catherine House and Honor Ayres.
　　p. cm.
　ISBN 0-8198-8312-3
1. Death--Religious aspects--Christianity--Juvenile literature.　I. Ayres, Honor. II. Title.
　BT825.H785 2007
　236'.1--dc22

2006014078

First edition, 2005

First North American Edition, 2007

Published by Pauline Books & Media, 50 Saint Paul's Avenue, Boston, MA 02130-3491. www.pauline.org

Printed and bound in Singapore

Pauline Books & Media is the publishing house of the Daughters of St. Paul, an international congregation of women religious serving the Church with the communications media.

1 2 3 4 5 6 7 8 9　　　　　　　　　　　　　　　　　14 13 12 11 10 09 08 07